365
ILLUSTRATED
MEDITATIONS

Mike Medaglia

To Lisa.
This journey of a thousand
miles began with you
by my side.

SELF MADE HERO

First published 2015
by SelfMadeHero
139-141 Pancras Road
London NW1 1UN
www.selfmadehero.com

Images copyright © 2015 Mike Medaglia
Illustrated by Mike Medaglia

Publishing Assistant: Guillaume Rater
Sales & Marketing Manager: Sam Humphrey
Publicist: Paul Smith
Publishing Director: Emma Hayley
Designer: Kate McLauchlan

A CIP record for this book is available from the British Library

ISBN: 978-1-910593-01-1

10 9 8 7 6 5 4 3 2

Printed and bound in Slovenia

INTRODUCTION

A good quote can change your outlook – if only for a second. It can give you hope, inspire change, make you laugh and remind you of the richness of life, all in a single sentence. That was my starting point for this book: to take words from the people that have inspired me, adapt them into illustrations that expressed their meaning and then share them with you!

With a page for every day of the year, you have a daily meditation to ponder and carry with you. When you wake up, you can grab this book and see what message awaits you. Maybe read each day's page at night before turning out the lights. Or at times you might just need a bit of inspiration and can open this book to read the words of great thinkers, artists, writers, activists and spiritual leaders. Sometimes the right words can come at the right time, exactly when they're needed.

I chose these meditations because they inspired me both artistically and spiritually. But more importantly they were all chosen because of their messages of hope, change, positivity and love.

I'd like to say thank you to my wife, Lisa Woynarski, to my parents for their endless support and to my sister, Melissa Medaglia, for finding me so many good quotes! A huge thank you also goes to Tim Hassan, Karrie Fransman, Hannah Berry, the Woynarskis, John Dunning, Steven Walsh, Andy Poyiadgi, Mauricio Molizane De Souza, Elena Jessup, Jessica Kingsley, Becca Hersey, Emma Carroll, Gosh! Comics, my editor Emma Hayley and all the folks at SelfMadeHero. A special thank you to Samar Hammam, for believing in me before I believed in myself.

Lastly, to you, the reader. May your year ahead be an inspired one!

Mike Medaglia

The ONLY journey is the one WITHIN.

RAINER MARIA RILKE

January 1

January 2

DWELL IN POSSIBILITY

EMILY DICKINSON

January 3

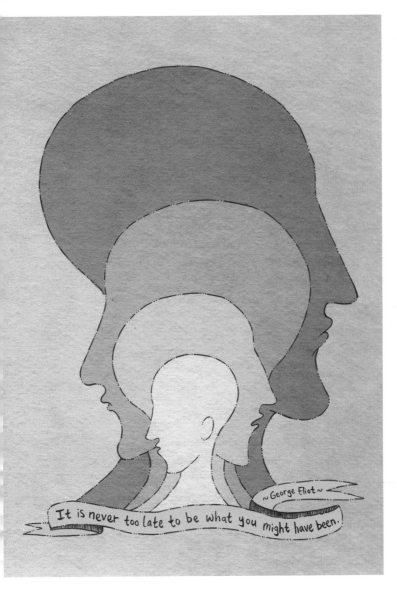

It is never too late to be what you might have been. ~George Eliot~

January 4

January 5

January 6

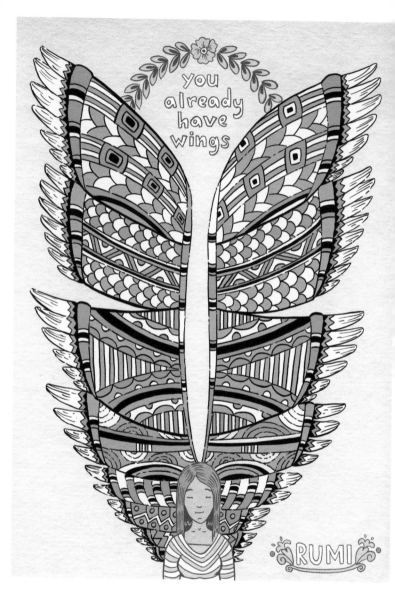

January 7

Dwell on the beauty of life. Watch the stars, and see yourself running with them.

~Marcus Aurelius~

January 8

January 9

January 10

One does not love one's children just because they are one's children but because of the friendship formed while raising them.

GABRIEL GARCIA MÁRQUEZ

January 11

The most common way people give up their power is by thinking they don't have any.

Alice Walker

January 12

If you hear a voice within you say you cannot paint, then by all means paint and that voice will be silenced.

Vincent van Gogh

January 13

January 14

Many people are alive but don't touch the miracle of being alive.

THICH NHAT HANH

January 15

January 16

January 17

January 18

January 19

January 20

January 21

January 22

January 23

January 24

January 25

The kindness we extend to others ripples out into the universe endlessly.

~Calvin Malone~

January 26

It's not the size of the dog in the fight,
it's the size of the fight in the dog.
~ Mark Twain ~

January 27

If you take a flower in your hand and really look at it, it's your world for the moment.

GEORGIA O'KEEFFE

January 28

FAILURE is imPOSSIBLE

SUSAN B. ANTHONY

January 29

January 30

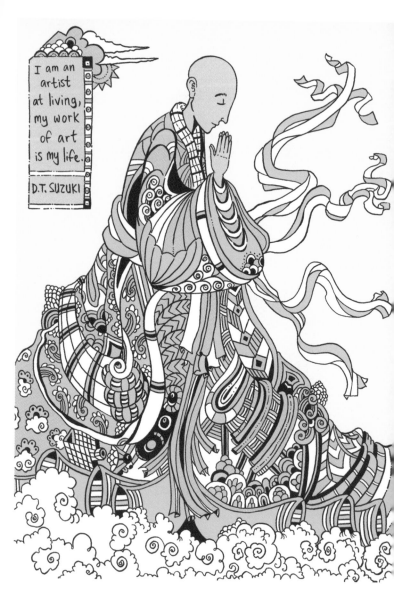

I am an
artist
at living,
my work
of art
is my life.

D.T. SUZUKI

January 31

February 1

February 2

February 3

February 4

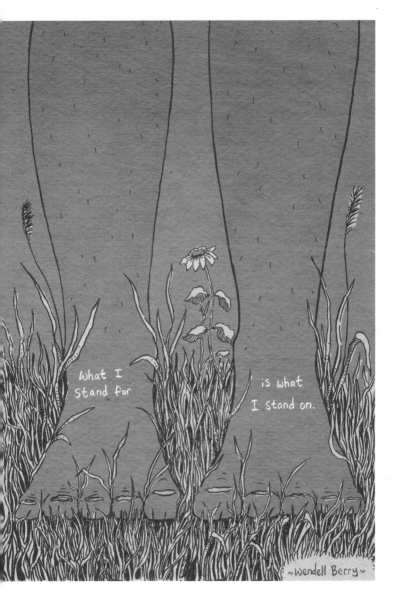

What I
Stand for

is what
I stand on.

~Wendell Berry~

February 5

Life is as dear to a mute creature as it is to man. Just as one wants happiness and fears pain, just as one wants to live and not die, so do other creatures.

~ DALAI LAMA XIV

February 6

February 7

February 8

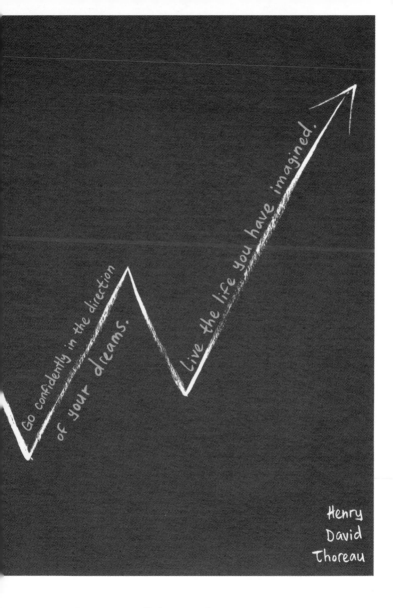

Go confidently in the direction of your dreams. Live the life you have imagined.

Henry David Thoreau

February 9

February 10

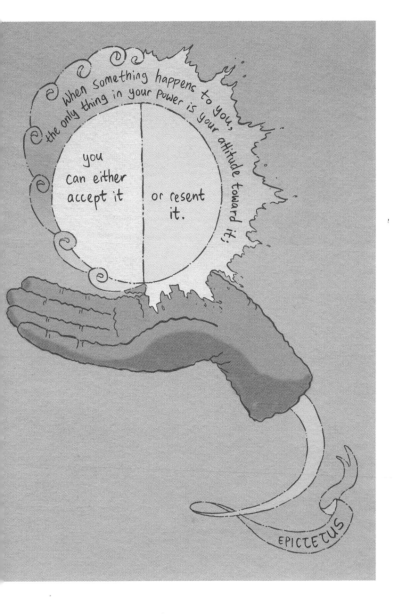

When something happens to you, the only thing in your power is your attitude toward it:
you can either accept it or resent it.

EPICTETUS

February 11

February 12

February 13

THERE IS
NO REMEDY

FOR
LOVE

BUT TO
LOVE MORE.

HENRY DAVID THOREAU

February 14

You work that you may keep pace with the earth and the soul of the earth.

For to be idle is to become a stranger unto the seasons and to step out of life's procession that marches in majesty and proud submission towards the infinite.

~KAHLIL GIBRAN~

February 15

February 16

IT IS ALWAYS
THE
SIMPLE

that
produces
the
MARVELOUS

AMELIA BARR

February 17

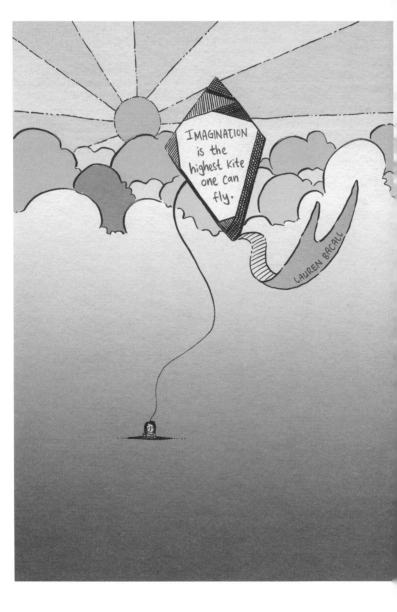

February 18

February 19

February 20

February 21

Let the beauty we love be what we do.

There are a hundred ways to kneel and kiss the earth.

~Rumi~

February 22

People suffer because they are caught in their views.

As soon as we release those views, we are free and we don't suffer anymore.

~THICH NHAT HANH

February 23

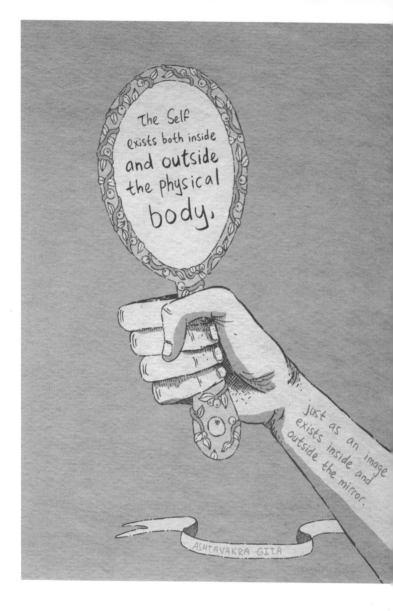

The Self exists both inside and outside the physical body,

just as an image exists inside and outside the mirror.

ASHTAVAKRA GITA

February 24

A happy
life is one
which is in
accord with its
own nature.

SENECA

February 25

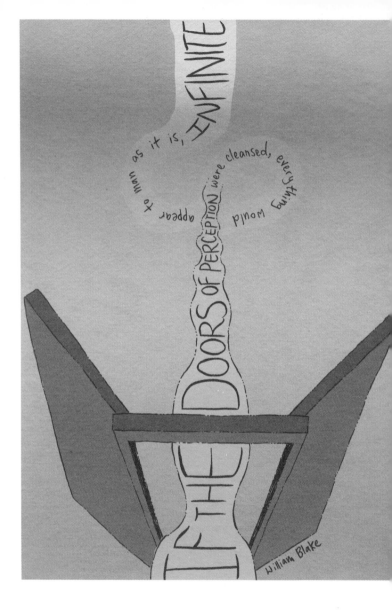

February 26

There are two ways of spreading light: to be the candle or the mirror that reflects it.

EDITH WHARTON

February 27

February 28

March 1

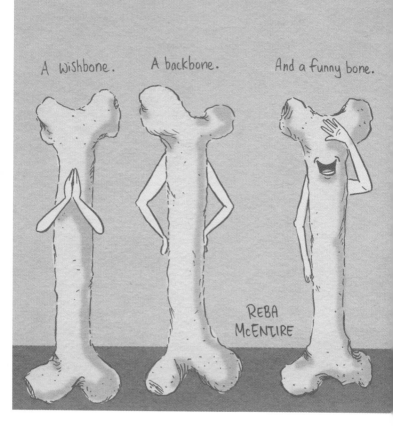

March 2

LIFE BEGETS A LIFE

ENERGY CREATES ENERGY

It is by spending ONESELF that one becomes RICH.

SARAH BERNHARDT

March 3

March 4

Reality is like a face reflected in the blade of a knife;

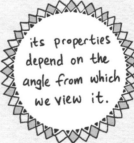

its properties depend on the angle from which we view it.

~Master Hsing Yun~

March 5

No one is useless in this world who lightens the burdens of another.

CHARLES DICKENS

March 6

March 7

March 8

March 9

March 10

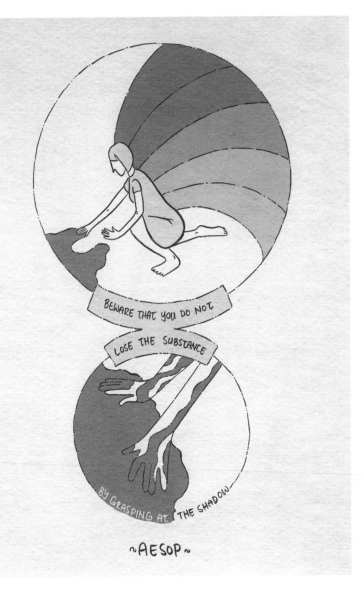

BEWARE THAT YOU DO NOT

LOSE THE SUBSTANCE

BY GRASPING AT THE SHADOW

~AESOP~

March 11

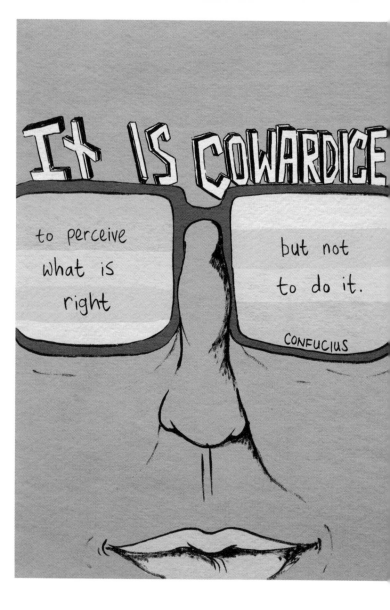

March 12

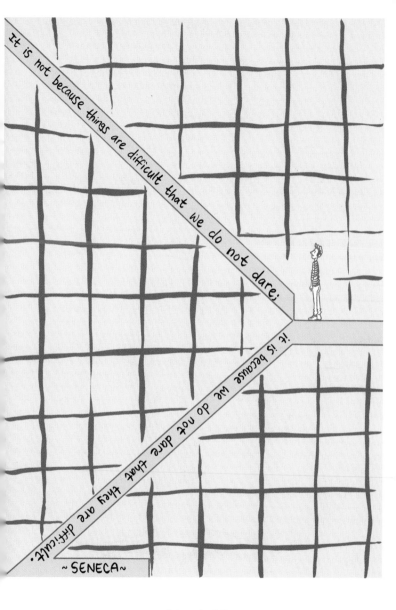

March 13

INTELLIGENCE IS THE ABILITY TO ADAPT TO CHANGE

STEPHEN HAWKING

March 14

March 15

Enlightenment is the mind which sees into impermanence.

DOGEN

March 16

March 17

If a thing loves, it is infinite.

WILLIAM BLAKE

March 18

March 19

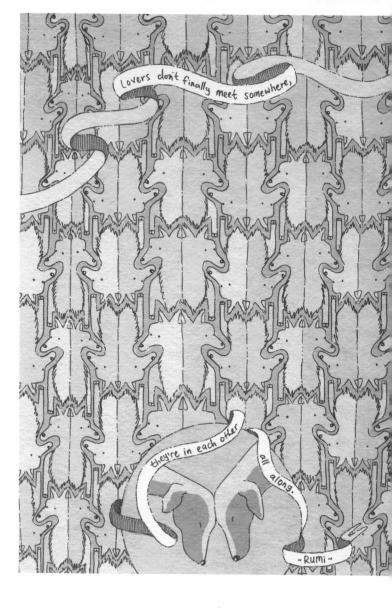

March 20

The beginning is always today.

MARY WOLLSTONECRAFT

March 21

It doesn't matter
   who you are
or what you look like,
so long as somebody
   loves you.

~ROALD DAHL~

March 22

FORGIVENESS

is
the key
to action
and
freedom.

~HANNAH ARENDT~

March 23

March 24

Life shrinks or expands in proportion to one's courage

ANAÏS NIN

March 25

March 26

March 27

Love dies

only when growth stops

Pearl S. Buck

March 28

Friendship is unnecessary, like philosophy, like art... it has no survival value; rather it is one of those things that give value to survival.

~C.S. Lewis~

March 30

March 31

April 1

To teach is to learn twice.

JOSEPH JOUBERT

April 2

Light tomorrow

with today.

Elizabeth Barrett Browning

April 3

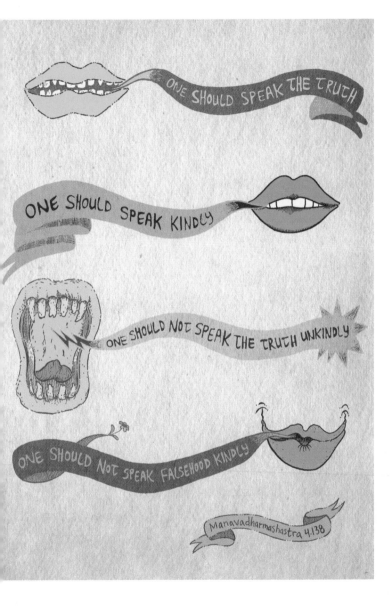

April 4

April 5

April 6

the interacting forces in nature generate artistic forms (water moves in swirls as waves crash and tumble down the banks of a river).

ANNA HALPRIN

April 7

April 8

April 9

Far away there in the sunshine are my highest aspirations. I may not reach them, but I can look up and see their beauty, believe in them, and try to follow where they lead.

~ Louisa May Alcott ~

April 10

April 11

April 12

April 13

April 14

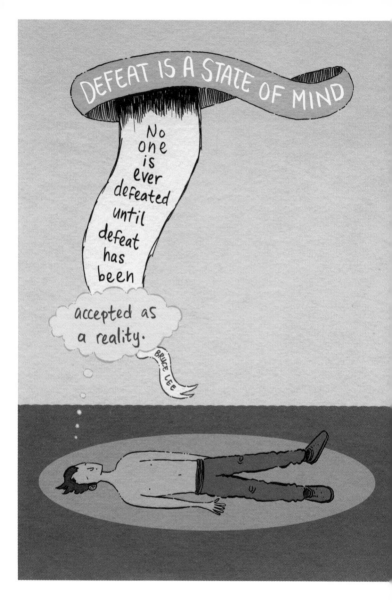

April 15

Tea is drunk to forget the din of the World.

Tien Yi-heng

April 16

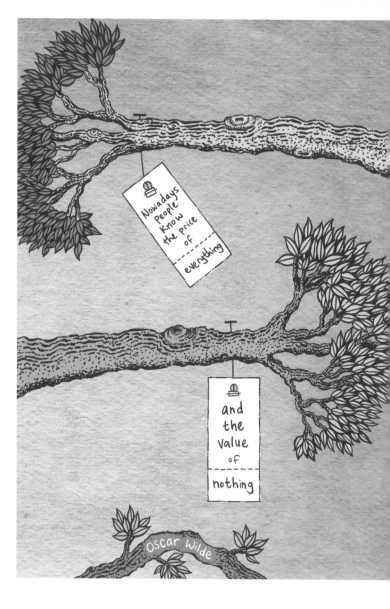

April 17

Healing is not an overnight process.

It is a daily cleansing of pain.

It is a daily healing of your life.

LEON BROWN

April 18

April 19

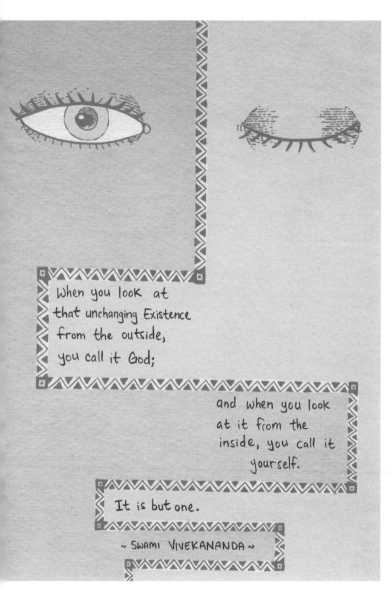

When you look at
that unchanging Existence
from the outside,
you call it God;

and when you look
at it from the
inside, you call it
yourself.

It is but one.

~ SWAMI VIVEKANANDA ~

April 20

We are not held back by the love we didn't receive in the past, but by the love we're not extending in the present.

MARIANNE WILLIAMSON

April 21

April 22

April 23

April 24

The worst prison would be a closed heart.

POPE JOHN PAUL II

April 25

April 26

April 27

To be fully alive, fully human and completely awake is to be continually thrown out of the nest.

PEMA CHÖDRÖN

April 28

April 29

April 30

May 1

If you don't find a teacher soon, you'll live this life in vain.

~ Bodhidharma

May 2

May 3

May 4

AS SOON AS YOU TRUST YOURSELF, YOU WILL KNOW HOW TO LIVE.

Johann Wolfgang von Goethe

May 5

the grand essentials to happiness in this life are

something to do,

Something to love

and something to hope for.

GEORGE WASHINGTON BURNAP

May 6

May 7

May 8

One must from time to time attempt things that are beyond one's capacity.

PIERRE-AUGUSTE RENOIR

May 9

The Moon's the same old moon, the flowers exactly as they were,

YET I'VE BECOME THE THINGNESS
OF ALL THE THINGS I SEE.

~BUNAN~

May 10

The Poetry of EARTH is NEVER dead

~ John Keats ~

May 11

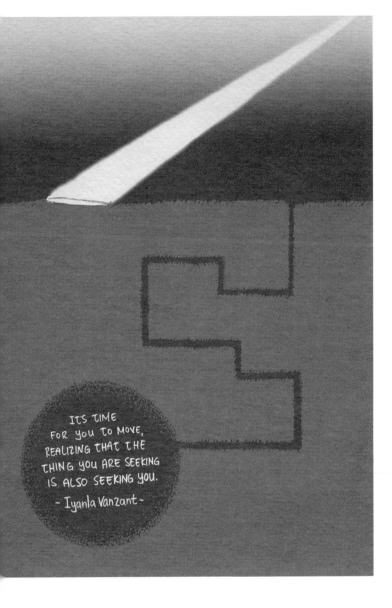

IT'S TIME
FOR YOU TO MOVE,
REALIZING THAT THE
THING YOU ARE SEEKING
IS ALSO SEEKING YOU.

- Iyanla Vanzant -

May 12

May 13

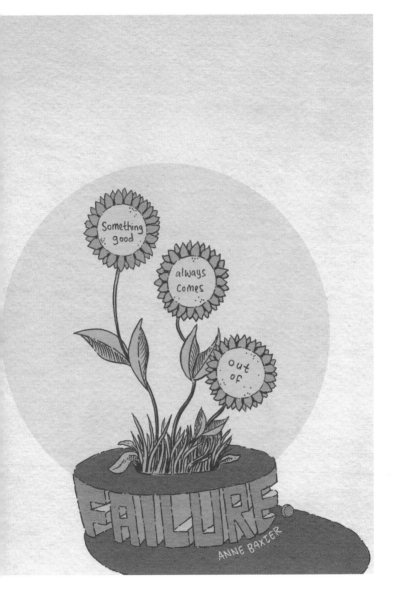

Something good always comes out of FAILURE.

ANNE BAXTER

May 14

May 15

We are but visitors on this planet. We are here for ninety or one hundred years at the very most. During that period, we must try to do something good, something useful with our lives. If you contribute to other people's happiness, you will find the true goal, the true meaning of life.

DALAI LAMA XIV

May 16

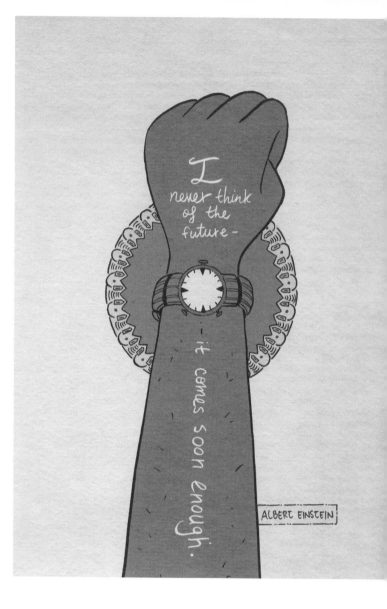

May 17

Set out from any point.

They are all alike.

They all lead to a point of departure.

~ANTONIO PORCHIA~

May 18

May 19

May 20

THE SUPREME HAPPINESS OF LIFE IS THE CONVICTION THAT WE ARE LOVED.

VICTOR HUGO

May 21

May 22

May 23

May 24

you are a
child of the universe
no less than the trees
and the stars; you have a
right to be here. And whether
or not it is clear to you,
no doubt the universe is
unfolding as it should.

MAX EHRMANN

May 25

May 26

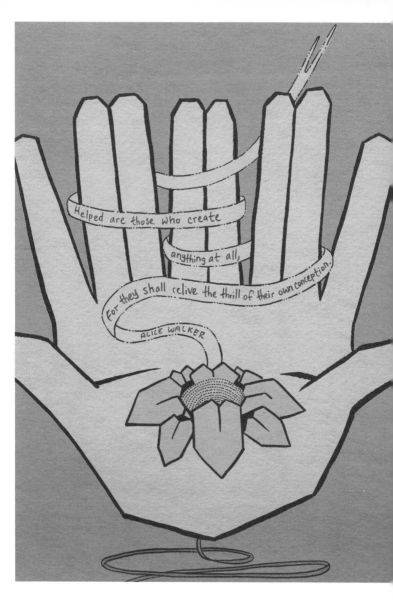

Helped are those who create anything at all, for they shall relive the thrill of their own conception.

ALICE WALKER

May 27

"GREATNESS"

exists in the inconspicuous and overlooked details.

LEONARD KOREN

May 28

The act of
meditation
is being
spacious.

~Sogyal Rinpoche~

May 29

May 30

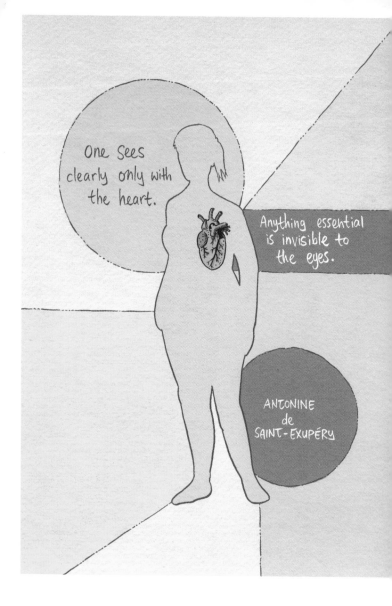

May 31

We can complain because rose bushes have thorns, or rejoice because thorn bushes have roses.

ABRAHAM LINCOLN

June 1

Without leaps of imagination, or dreaming, we lose the excitement of possibilities. Dreaming, after all, is a form of planning.

☙GLORIA STEINEM❧

June 2

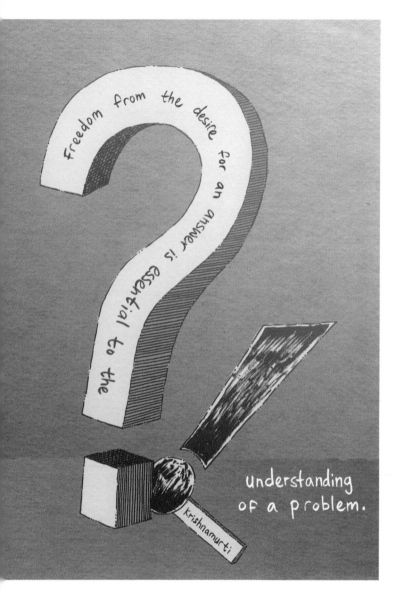

Freedom from the desire for an answer is essential to the understanding of a problem.

krishnamurti

June 3

ANGER is the ULTIMATE destroyer of your own peace of mind.

DALAI LAMA XIV

June 4

June 5

June 6

Change the way you look at things and the things you look at Change.

Wayne Dyer

June 7

June 9

June 10

Of all **strategies,** knowing when to

QUIT

may be the best.

Chinese proverb

June 11

The FUTURE

is made of the same stuff as the

PRESENT

Simone Weil

June 13

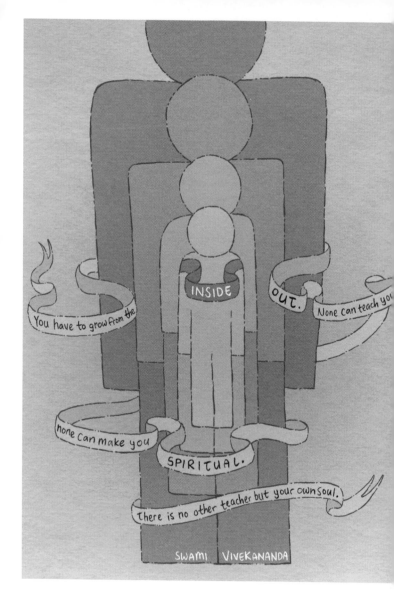

You have to grow from the INSIDE OUT. None can teach you, none can make you SPIRITUAL. There is no other teacher but your own soul.

SWAMI VIVEKANANDA

June 14

June 15

June 16

June 17

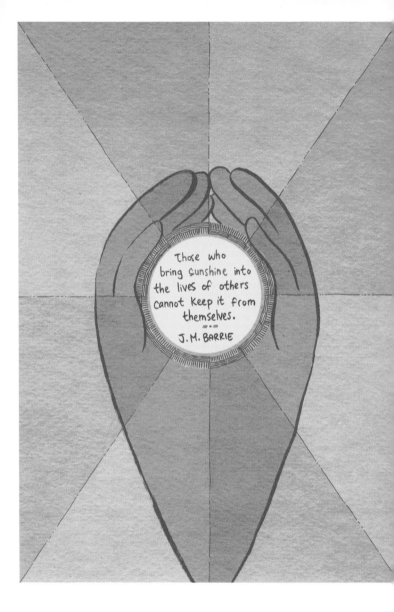

Those who
bring sunshine into
the lives of others
cannot keep it from
themselves.
=•=
J. M. BARRIE

June 18

June 19

June 20

June 21

June 22

Each season is but an infinitesimal point.

It no sooner comes than it is gone.

It has no duration.

It simply gives a tone and hue to my thought.

HENRY DAVID THOREAU

June 23

One joy scatters a hundred griefs.

Chinese Proverb

June 24

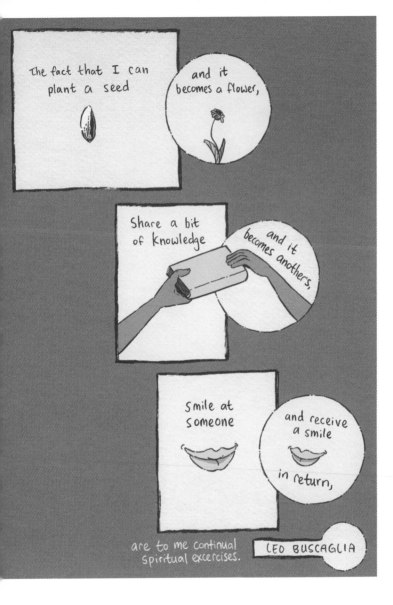

June 25

June 26

There are years that ask questions and years that answer.

ZORA NEALE HURSTON

June 27

True love cannot be found where it truly does not exist,
nor can it be hidden where it truly does.

François de La Rochefoucauld

June 28

At first you are awed by the splendour, by the beauty, of the planet

and then you look down and you realise that this one planet is the only thing we have.

JULIE PAYETTE

June 29

June 30

July 1

July 2

July 3

Well-behaved
Women seldom
make history.

LAUREL THATCHER ULRICH

July 4

July 5

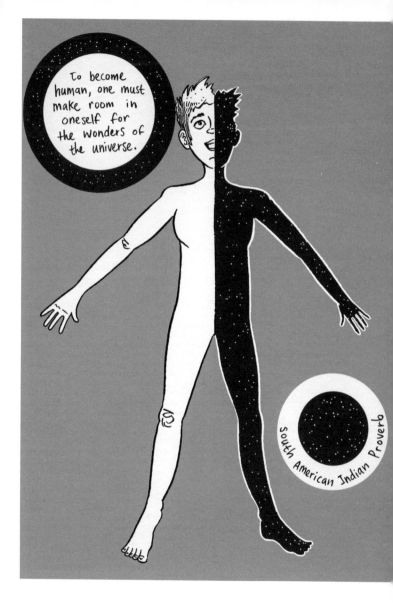

July 6

July 7

July 8

July 9

July 10

July 11

July 12

Never underestimate the power of dreams

and the influence of the human Spirit.

We are all the same in this notion: the potential for greatness lives within each of us.

WILMA RUDOLPH

July 14

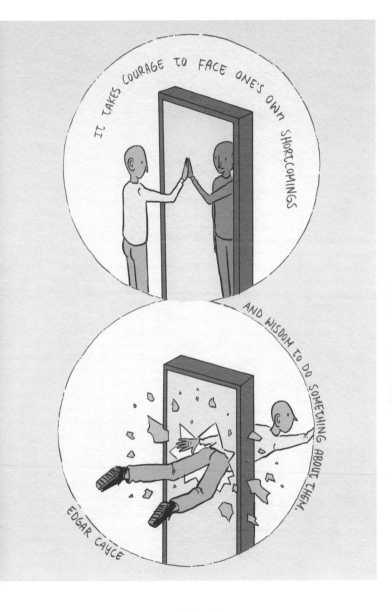

July 15

July 16

July 17

July 18

The way to overcome something is not to avoid it but to move into it.

~ Arnie Kozak ~

July 19

July 20

July 21

July 22

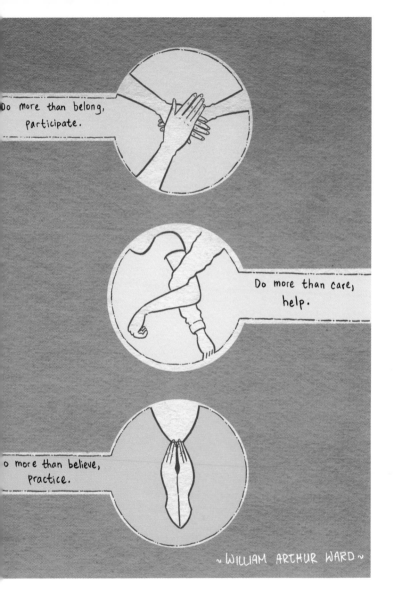

Do more than belong,
Participate.

Do more than care,
help.

Do more than believe,
Practice.

~ WILLIAM ARTHUR WARD ~

July 23

July 24

The more clearly we can focus our attention on the wonders and realities of the universe about us,

THE LESS TASTE WE SHALL HAVE FOR DESTRUCTION

RACHEL CARSON

July 25

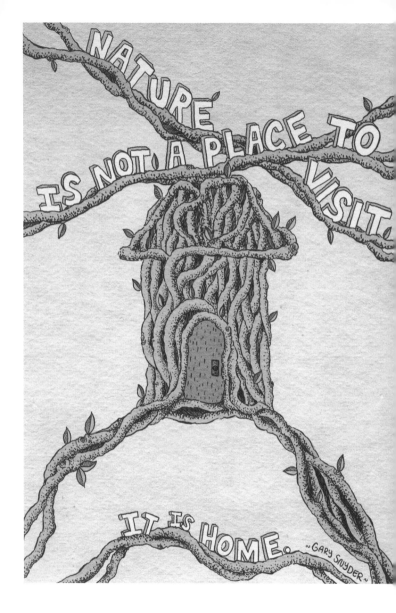

July 26

July 27

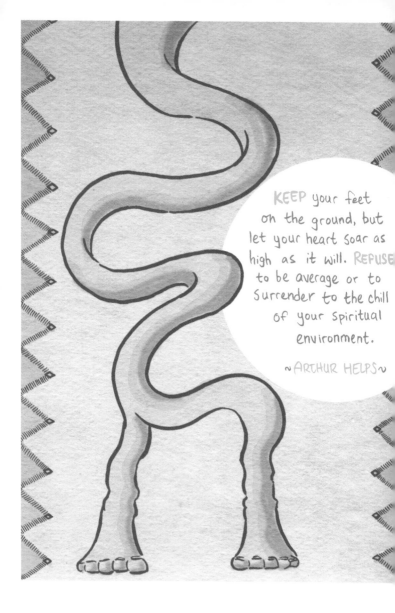

July 28

The only person you are destined to become is the person you decide to be.

RALPH WALDO EMERSON

July 29

July 30

July 31

August 1

August 2

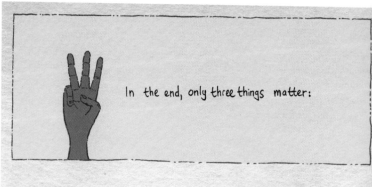

In the end, only three things matter:

How much you loved,

how gently you lived,

you lived,

and how gracefully you let go of things not meant for you.

~ Jack Kornfield ~

August 3

August 4

Happiness makes up in height
what it lacks in length.

~ Robert Frost

August 5

August 6

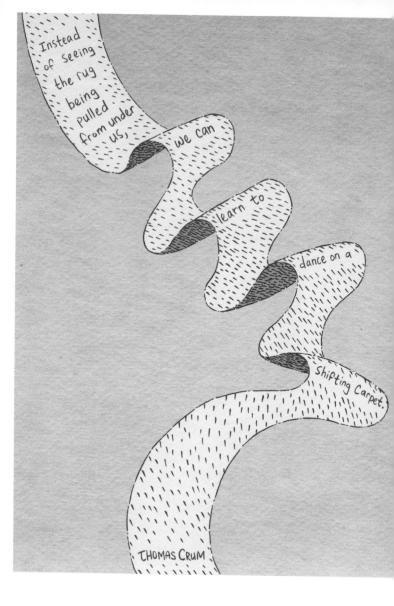

Instead of seeing the rug being pulled from under us, we can learn to dance on a shifting carpet.

THOMAS CRUM

August 7

Think lightly of yourself and deeply of the world.

MIYAMOTO MUSASHI

August 8

THE HIGHEST

RESULT

OF EDUCATION

IS TOLERANCE

HELEN KELLER

August 9

August 10

August 11

August 12

when the gods wish to punish us, they answer our prayers.

OSCAR WILDE

August 13

There is no passion to be found in playing small – in settling for a life that is less than the one you are capable of living.

NELSON MANDELA

August 14

August 15

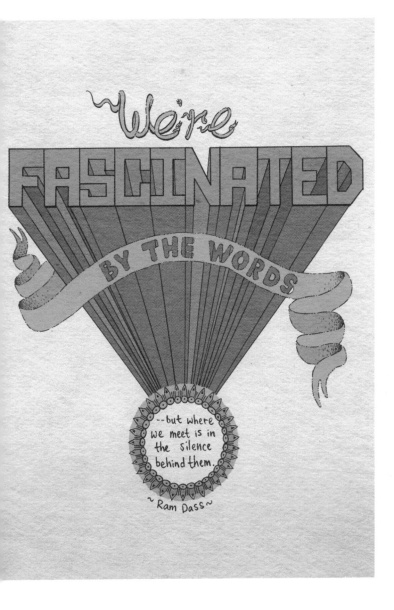

We're FASCINATED BY THE WORDS

--but where we meet is in the silence behind them.

~Ram Dass~

August 16

August 17

August 18

August 19

August 20

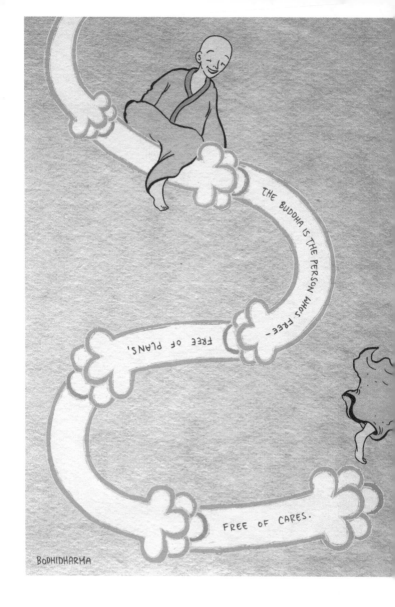

August 21

The respect that is only brought by GOLD is not worth Much.

FRANCES E.W. HARPER

August 22

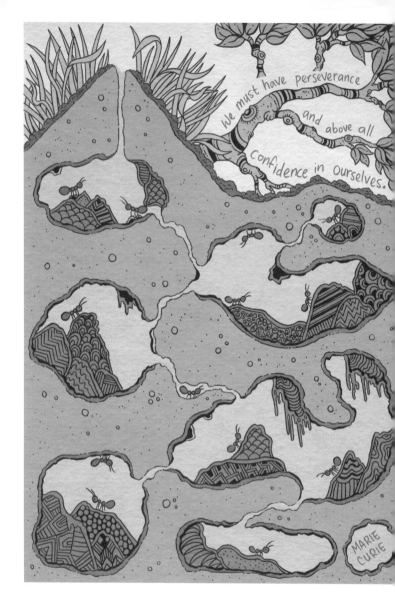

August 23

What is a friend?

A single soul dwelling in two bodies.

~ARISTOTLE~

August 24

August 25

August 26

August 27

August 28

August 29

PERHAPS WE CANNOT RAISE THE WINDS. BUT EACH OF US CAN PUT UP THE SAIL, SO THAT WHEN THE WIND COMES WE CAN CATCH IT.

E.F. SCHUMACHER

August 30

August 31

To be loved means to be recognized as existing.

THICH NHAT HANH

September 1

If we did all the things we are capable of doing, we would

LITERALLY ASTOUND OURSELVES

THOMAS A. EDISON

September 2

September 3

September 4

Certain things catch your eye, but pursue only those that capture your **HEART**

Native American Proverb

September 5

September 6

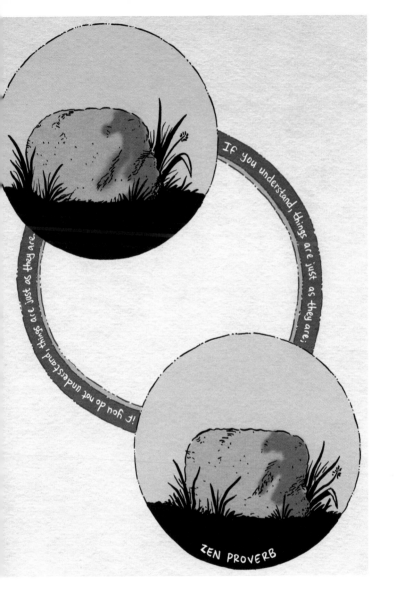

If you understand, things are just as they are; if you do not understand, things are just as they are.

ZEN PROVERB

September 7

TO BE ALIVE IN THIS BEAUTIFUL, SELF-ORGANIZING UNIVERSE --
TO PARTICIPATE IN THE DANCE OF LIFE WITH SENSES TO PERCEIVE
IT, LUNGS TO BREATHE IT, ORGANS THAT DRAW NOURISHMENT
FROM IT -- IS A WONDER BEYOND WORDS.

JOANNA MACY

September 8

September 9

CONSTANT EFFORT and FREQUENT MISTAKES are the STEPPING STONES of

= ELBER

September 10

September 11

You can often change your circumstances by changing your attitude.

ELEANOR ROOSEVELT

September 12

A book is a door, you know.

Always
and
forever.

A book is a door into another place

and another heart

and another world.

~Catherynne M. Valente~

September 13

September 14

September 15

September 16

September 17

September 18

September 19

September 20

September 21

September 22

September 23

September 24

September 25

September 26

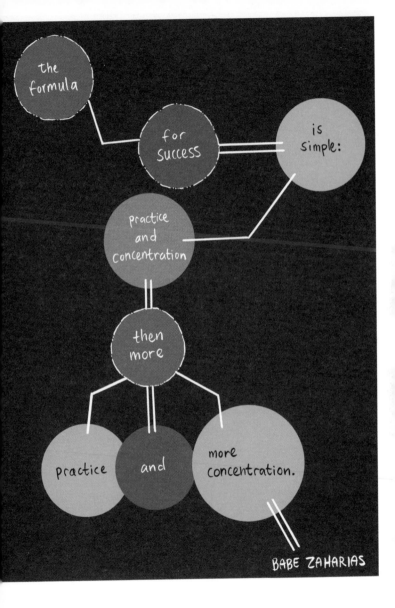

September 27

September 28

September 29

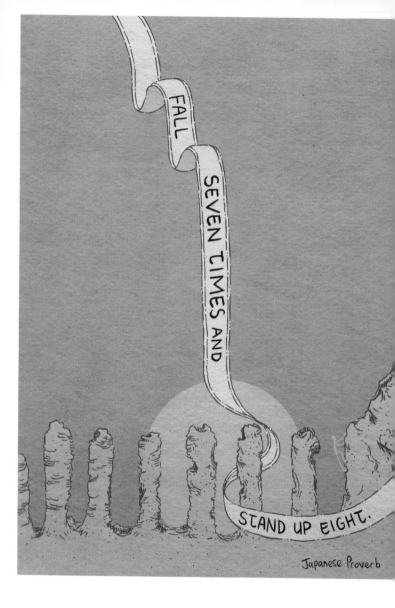

FALL SEVEN TIMES AND STAND UP EIGHT.

Japanese Proverb

September 30

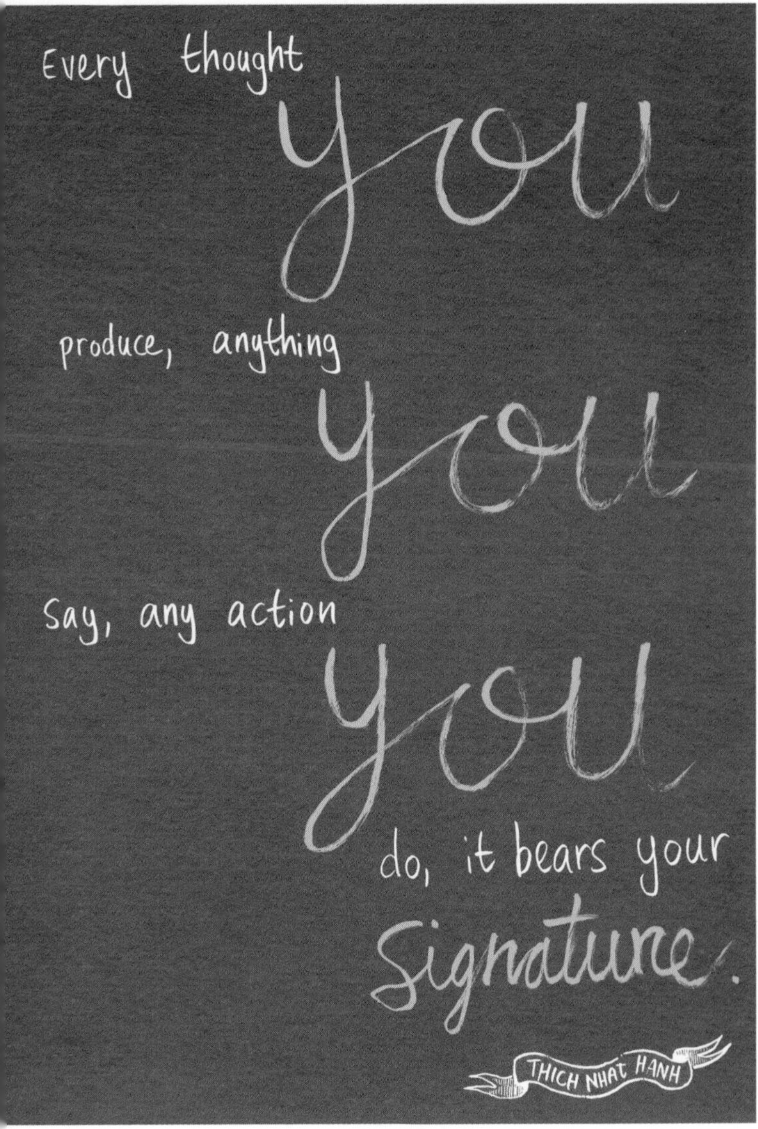

Every thought *you* produce, anything *you* say, any action *you* do, it bears your *signature*.

THICH NHAT HANH

October 1

October 2

October 3

October 4

October 5

October 6

October 7

Follow through on all your generous IMPULSES

EPICTETUS

October 8

Generosity is the essence of friendship.

OSCAR WILDE

October 9

October 10

October 11

October 12

October 13

October 14

October 15

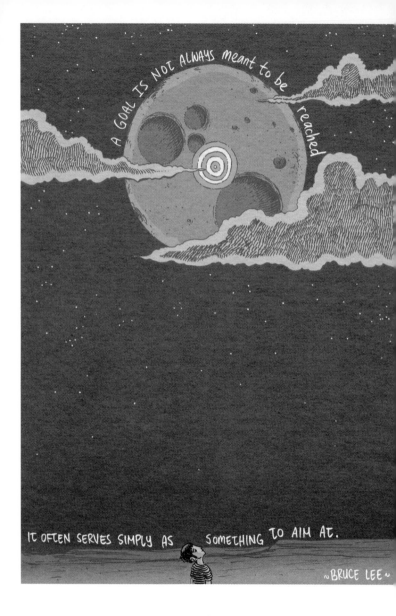

October 16

October 17

October 18

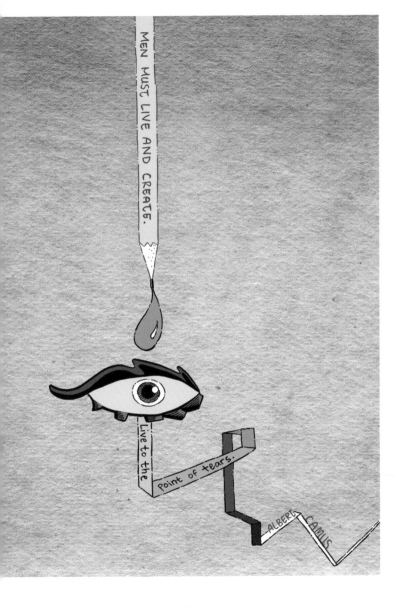

MEN MUST LIVE AND CREATE.

Live to the point of tears.

ALBERT CAMUS

October 19

October 20

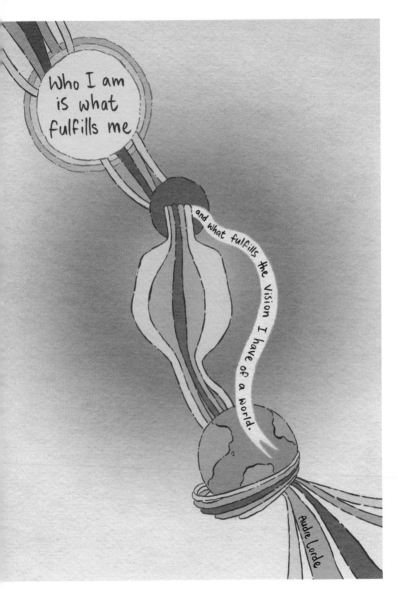

October 21

October 22

October 23

October 24

October 25

The Best Way to Cheer yourself **up** is to try to cheer someone else **up**.

~Mark Twain~

October 26

Time Discovers Truth. ~SENECA~

October 27

TROUBLE is part of your life - if you don't share it, you don't give the person who loves you a chance to love you enough.

DINAH SHORE

October 28

October 29

October 30

Someday I'll be a weather-beaten skull resting on a grass pillow, Serenaded by a stray bird or two.

Kings and commoners end up the same, No more enduring than last night's dream.

~Ryōkan

October 31

November 1

November 2

November 3

November 4

November 5

Concealing shortcomings while boasting virtue defines arrogance.

~Miao-lo~

November 6

November 7

November 8

I would rather die of passion than of boredom.

VINCENT VAN GOGH

November 9

November 10

November 11

November 12

November 13

When you get into a tight place and everything goes against you until it seems that you cannot hold on for a minute longer, never give up then, for that is just the place and time when the tide will turn.

HARRIET BEECHER STOWE

November 14

November 15

November 16

November 17

November 18

November 19

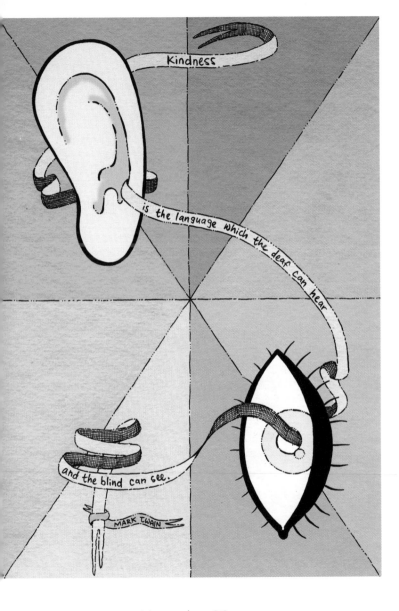

November 20

November 21

November 22

November 23

November 24

Be faithful in small things because it is in them that your strength lies.

MOTHER TERESA

November 25

Fulfillment of desire is an illusion; desire leads to more desire, not satisfaction.

~ Kathleen McDonald ~

November 26

November 27

you Only live once,

BUT IF YOU DO IT RIGHT, ONCE IS ENOUGH.

MAE WEST

November 28

BECAUSE EACH EXISTENCE IS IN CONSTANT CHANGE, THERE IS NO ABIDING SELF.

SHUNRYU SUZUKI

November 29

November 30

If the whole universe can be found in our own body and mind, this is where we need to make our inquiries. ~Ayya Khema~

December 1

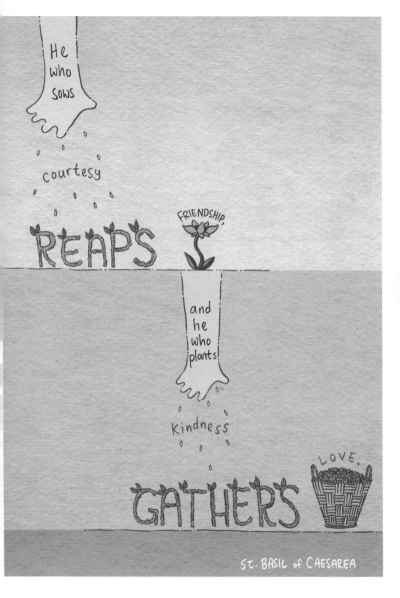

December 2

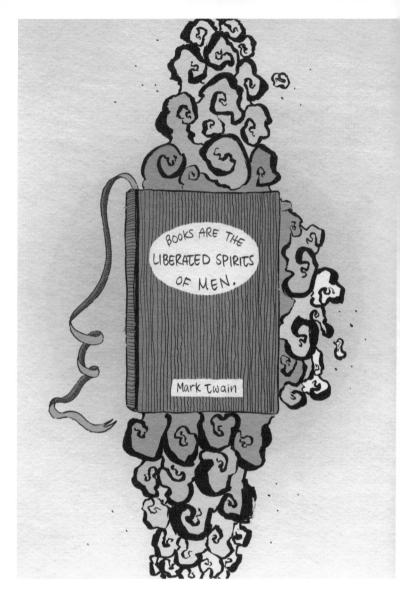

December 3

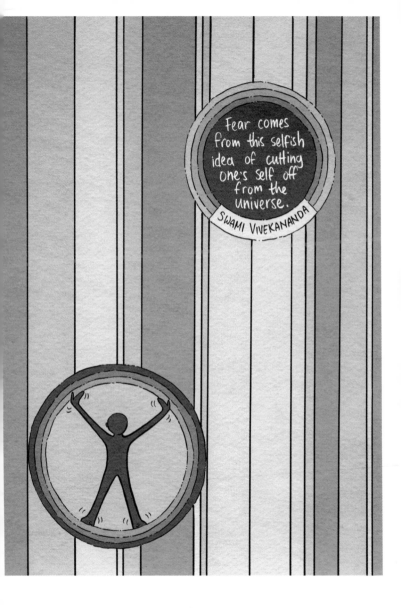

Fear comes from this selfish idea of cutting one's self off from the universe.

SWAMI VIVEKANANDA

December 4

December 5

AND THE DAY CAME WHEN THE RISK TO REMAIN tight in a bud was more painful than the risk it took to blossom.

ANAÏS NIN

December 6

December 7

Knowledge comes,
but wisdom lingers.

Alfred Tennyson

December 8

December 9

You are not Atlas carrying the world on your shoulder.

It is good to remember that the planet is carrying you.

Vandana Shiva

December 10

December 11

December 12

We may need permission, from time to time, to allow ourselves to relax, to not be so hard on ourselves- to simply be at ease and happy. We need to learn to be kind to ourselves.

CHÖKYI NYIMA RINPOCHE

December 13

December 14

Our life is frittered away by detail.

~ Henry David Thoreau ~

December 15

It is only possible to live

happily ever after

on a day to day basis.

MARGARET BONANNO

December 16

December 17

December 18

The truth is on the MARCH and nothing will stop it.

EMILE ZOLA

December 19

We are all gifted.
That is our inheritance.
• ETHEL WATERS •

December 20

December 21

There is always
something left
to love.

GABRIEL
GARCIA
MÁRQUEZ

December 22

December 23

December 24

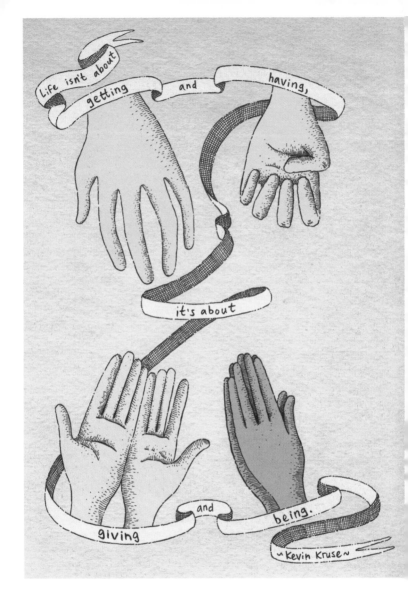

Life isn't about getting and having, it's about giving and being.

~Kevin Kruse~

December 25

the purpose of life is to be defeated by greater and greater things.
~ Rainer Maria Rilke ~

December 26

December 27

December 28

December 29

December 30

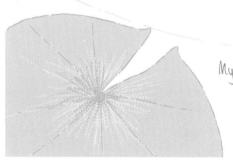

Flowers as they are

In the lotus pond:

My offering to the spirits.

~ Matsuo Bashō ~

December 31